DRIVE THRU SUCCESS

Finding Success While Waiting in the Drive Thru

ROBERT B. WALKER

Foreword by Bobby Jones & David Thompson

Drive Thru Success

Visit the web site at **www.drivethrusuccess.com** or

Tweet with us on **twitter.com/drivethrusucces**

Copyright © 2010 by Sports Spectrum Publishing

Design by Renata Bolden

Edited by Brett Honeycutt

All rights reserved. No portion of this book may be reproduced, stored in a retrieval system, or transmitted in any form or by any means – electronic, mechanical, recording, scanning, or other except for brief quotation in printed reviews, without the prior permission of the publisher.

The Core Media Group Inc.

P.O. Box 2037

Indian Trail, NC 28079

Art Copyright © Getty Images

Bible quotations, unless otherwise noted, are taken from the HOLY BIBLE, NEW INTERNATIONAL VERSION. Copyright © 1973, 1978, 1984, International Bible Society. Used by permission of Zondervan Bible Publishers.

CONTENTS

	Foreword by Bobby Jones and David Thompson ...	**IX**
	Acknowledgements.....................................	**XIII**
	Introduction	**XV**
Chapter 1	Jump In	1
Chapter 2	The Ride	7
Chapter 3	The Menu	13
Chapter 4	May I Take Your Order	19
Chapter 5	Waiting in Line	25
Chapter 6	The Window	31
Chapter 7	Here's Your Order	39
Chapter 8	Thank You!	45
Chapter 9	Oops! Too Much Change	51
Chapter 10	Drive Away	57
	Drive Thru Steps to Success	63
	Drive Thru Success Extra: Renewing the Mind	67
	About The Author	86
	Reader's Quotes	88

Drive Thru Success

*This book is dedicated to
all of those serving others
through the fast food
and restaurant industries*

FOREWORD BY BOBBY JONES

In 1972, as a rising junior at the University of North Carolina at Chapel-Hill, I had the honor of representing the United States by playing on the Olympic basketball team in the XX Olympics in Munich, Germany. While this was a high point in my basketball career, the 37 years since those events have altered many of our memories of how things really were. This was brought to my attention recently when two writers interviewed me about my experiences during that time. They were in the process of interviewing each participant on that team for an upcoming book. The writers were surprised at how so many different recollections of the same event could come forth from the interviewees. The passage of time, the desire to shape a memory the way we want, and the filling of our minds with other experiences can distort what really took place in our past experiences. Fortunately, the God who created our world is not encumbered by those limitations and knows precisely what happened and why. How we live our lives is a testament to the thankfulness we have to our Creator as we seek to honor Him through our daily actions. We see this in 2 Corinthians 10:5, which says: "We demolish arguments and every pretension that sets itself up against the knowledge of God, and we take captive every thought to make it obedient to Christ." While this is our goal, we fall short of that directive given by the apostle Paul.

I have known Robert Walker for more than 20 years, having worked with, vacationed with, gone on mission trips with, and competed with him during that time. A man of high energy and a positive outlook on life, Robert's endearing quality is walking through life knowing that God is in on every meeting, discussion, and event.

He is bold in his faith to share the good news with those he comes in contact. In *Drive Thru Success*, Robert has put together some basic reminders for how we are to live our lives in obedience to God. Robert's take on the simple process of going through a drive thru restaurant correlates to how we can be effective in various situations in our own lives. From jumping into the car to driving away with food in hand, each chapter presents an opportunity to do things the right way.

While the decade may change how we remember events, the truth of doing things the right way can and will give us a peace in knowing that we have tried to honor God through the life He has given to each of us.

FOREWORD BY DAVID THOMPSON

I first met Robert Walker almost two decades ago. I was asked to play in a fantasy basketball camp in Hawaii, along with Bobby Jones, and Robert negotiated my appearance fee. He did such a great job that I asked him to represent me on a permanent basis. Over the years, we've developed a great relationship. He is a hard worker, dedicated family man, strong Christian, and an honest, loyal friend. He's not only been a friend to me, but to my wife Cathy and daughters Erika and Brooke. I have watched Robert grow his company using the same principles he talks about in *Drive Thru Success*.

The chapter, The Menu, talks about accepting new challenges with an opportunistic attitude, and also overcoming life's challenges that we have no control over. This chapter touched me because it is relevant to my life. I've realized that the most difficult thing for anyone is change; sometimes we will stay in a bad situation because it's familiar or comfortable. However, we all know with God that we can overcome all challenges.

Drive Thru Success is a great book that applies to anyone's life, be it business or personal.

ACKNOWLEDGEMENTS

To all of my current and former staff at Unlimited Success Sports Management and Sports Spectrum Magazine: Thank you Sharon Wade, Renata Bolden, Lindsay Adams, Ryan DiNunzio, Brett Honeycutt, Jenelle Jonkman, Brian Payne, Kristin Martin, and Aaron May, for helping me with things everyday in our business, and especially for your extra effort on this project. It seems like we are never without new projects. Thank you for your patience and understanding.

To my mother and father, Doug and Louise Walker, for helping to raise me in a faith-based, Christ-centered home. Home is always a pleasant place to be, and I guess you could say that all of those spankings worked after all. I want to thank my three brothers for being my friends and teammates as we grew up playing football, baseball, basketball, soccer or any other sport in the backyard. Those are fond memories.

To all the athletes I have had the privilege to work with over two decades. I have learned much from you, and it has been my honor and blessing to serve you.

To all the players I coached and had contact with while coaching soccer, basketball, and baseball, you helped me gain a greater understanding about patience and perseverance. Thank you.

To my business friends and associates who taught me so much about relationships, trust, and the heart of giving.

And to my beautiful, sweet wife Jacqueline and children Hannah and Matthew, thank you for your patience - listening to all my new ideas and thoughts, and for allowing me the time to pursue many different ways to help others.

And a very special thank you to all restaurants located near my office, which were part of the inspiration for this book: Arby's, Biscuitville, Bojangle's, Burger King, Chick-fil-A, Cook Out, Domino's, Dunkin' Donuts, East 74, Firehouse Subs, Hardee's, Johnny K's, Kentucky Fried Chicken, Krispy Kreme Doughnuts, Little Ceasar's, McDonald's, NY Pizza and Pasta, Panera Bread, Sonic Drive-In, Subway, Taco Bell, and Wendy's.

INTRODUCTION

The idea of *Drive Thru Success* came to me one day while sitting in my office preparing for a speech. I was scheduled to speak at a university and was brainstorming possible topics that would connect with college students. We all know that attention spans have grown shorter over the years and I needed something to keep their focus. I had a couple of topics that I really liked, but I felt like they lacked that connection; something everyone in the audience has experienced and understands. I wanted to speak to them about success and what exactly true success is.

As I began to think, my office location came to mind. Within a few blocks, there are many fast food restaurants. I can get hamburgers, hot dogs, French fries, roast beef, subs, fried chicken, baked chicken, chicken sandwiches, biscuits, tacos, burritos, pizza and more! I love the location of my office; I am in fast food heaven! As I began to connect the dots, I saw that much could be learned about true success while going through the drive thru. Each step of the drive thru experience represents a different step for success. Wow! This topic could connect with just about anyone: young or old, student or professor, incredibly wealthy or those just getting by. Everyone has been through a drive thru at least once. I knew this story could connect with those college students, and many others!

So one summer day, when my wife and kids were out of town, I stayed home from work and began writing it all down. With that, *Drive Thru Success* was born!

This book was meant to be short; I wanted to keep it consistent with the drive thru experience. So enjoy the ride, and discover what is sure to make an impact on your life and others: *Drive Thru Success.* Now let's jump in!

Drive Thru Success

Chapter 1

Jump In

"All mankind is divided into three classes: those that are immovable, those that are movable, and those that move."
Benjamin Franklin

Your Drive Thru experience will never get started if you don't jump into the car. If you really want something in life, you have to make a decision to jump in and make it happen. Have you ever thought about where you would be if you did not jump into your job everyday? What if you gave a half-hearted effort at work by missing deadlines, ignoring emails, surfing the web all day, or daydreaming during meetings? This lackadaisical effort could lead to missing out on a promotion, a raise, or, conversely, having your name placed first in line for layoffs.

Jumping in takes action. I'm not saying to casually think about something for weeks and months as opportunity passes you by, but instead, jump in! In life, you cannot be successful without accepting some level of risk. Whether you are single or married, college or high school student, parent or grandparent, we all need to jump in to make a difference. Think about what you need to jump into today:

- Spend more time with family
- Continue your education
- Spend more time practicing
- Be more proactive at work
- Find ways to help your community & world
- Get involved in your church
- Study harder
- Be a lifelong learner
- Consider a career change

I remember when I was an athletic director of a private school in Charlotte, NC. It was a great job, and we accomplished a lot in a short period of time. We built a new stadium for football and soccer, along with a state-of-the-art weight training facility. We also developed winning programs in baseball, football, soccer and basketball (which I had the privilege of serving as assistant head coach for two state titles). I was an athletic director from 1988-1994, but in 1993 I began to evaluate making a career change. I had started my own part-time business in 1988, but I wanted to be in business for myself full-time. I felt like I had accomplished what I was hired to do and was ready for a new challenge. I did not have any capital or anyone to invest in my new venture. I did, however, have enough money to cover my expenses for two months; the months of June and July.

Many people tried to convince me to stay at the school. I had a stable job, salary, benefits and friends. It would have been easy to stay. But after weighing my options, I went with my heart and jumped in. In June of 1994, I began running my business full-time. Has the road been easy? No, not at all. Is it fulfilling? Absolutely. If you would have told me in June of 1994 of the things I would do and the people I would meet, I would not have believed it. So I ask, what do you need to jump into today? Remember, I did not ask you to stick your toe in the pond. I said, JUMP IN! Go make your own splash!

Action Items

Write down some areas you want to jump into, then write out a timeline to make that jump.

Jump In

1.)

2.)

Timeline

1.)

2.)

"The greater danger for most of us lies not in setting our aim too high and falling short; but in setting our aim too low, and achieving our mark."

Michelangelo

Chapter 2

The Ride

"Treasure your relationships, not your possessions."

Anthony J. D'Angelo

Well now that we have jumped into the car, we begin the ride to our destination: the drive-thru. There are so many different kinds of automobiles; BMW, Chevrolet, Subaru, Volvo, Ford, Lexus, Toyota, Kia, Hyundai, Nissan, Honda, Jeep, Buick, Audi, Mercedes, Suzuki, Volkswagen... And each brand has many different models. Do we really need that many choices? We can only drive one car at a time, right? Well, the reason we have so many brands and models is because people are so different.

Everyone has their own taste and thoughts about an automobile. I have a Volvo and a Ford. Both vehicles are comfortable, have proven to be very reliable, and give me plenty of room for my family and my sports gear. But at the end of the day, it's not what I drive, it's the ride that's important. I need something to get me from point A to point B. If it's a BMW 7 Series, okay. If it's a 1971 Ford Pinto (considered by Time Magazine as one of the worst cars ever made) that's okay as well. So many times in life, we get caught up in what we have or what we don't have.

I remember one time when I had a gentleman come to my office for a meeting. He wanted to have lunch and talk about doing business together. I was all for it. A free lunch and the start of a new relationship make a great outing. When he arrived, I walked outside and noticed he had an old truck. It was not an antique, but it was definitely old. What stood out to me, though, was that it was clean and extremely neat. Even though he did not have the nicest car, he made it look the best it could, and that made a positive impression on me.

I even took a moment during our ride to compliment him on how clean his truck was, and it made him feel good that I took notice. You see, he was starting his own new venture and was investing in that instead of driving a status symbol. That told me he was a frugal businessman and wanted what was best for his clients first, not himself. Different things will carry you through life. The automobile will carry us to the drive thru, but it will not carry us to success.

Something or somebody will help carry us through life. You cannot make it through life alone. Sometimes the ride of life will be smooth, full of joy and happiness. Other times the ride will be bumpy, with adversity and hardship along the way. We have to find ways to balance the ride.

Have you ever ridden in a car where the tires are unbalanced or the front end is out of line? If so, you know the car is unstable and sometimes difficult to maneuver. However, if you take it to the shop, you can get it repaired. Then your ride will be so smooth you feel like you are floating down the street.

When my ride through life is bumpy, there is one place I can go to get a total repair - God's repair shop. The price is right because His repairs are free and His shop is open 24/7; no appointments necessary. When your life gets bumpy, where do you go to get repairs? I encourage you to check out God's repair shop. It has always worked for me.

We can make our ride significantly better, or worse, based on the choices we make along the ride of life. The challenges in life will make you want to stop. But if you stop, you will never get to the end of the drive thru to get what you want. Though it is okay to pause along the way and reflect, then push forward again. The drive thru has a lot of pauses. You hardly ever drive through without having to pause as the person in front of you makes their selection and picks up their order.

Along the ride of life, make the choice to never stop, never give up and never give in. You may pause, pray, think, and evaluate your choices - but never give up on the ride of life. Because as soon as you quit, you may miss out on the blessing just around the corner.

Action Items

Take a moment and reflect on what path you are riding on.
Write down three ways to repair or improve the ride you are currently on.

1.)

2.)

3.)

"Never give in, never give in, never; never; never; never – in nothing, great or small, large or petty – never give in except to convictions of honor and good sense."

Winston Churchill

Chapter 3

The Menu

"Don't fear failure so much that you refuse to try new things. The saddest summary of a life contains three descriptions: could have, might have, and should have."

Louis E. Boone

Our ride has now brought us to the drive thru menu. Have you ever taken a moment to count all the items on the drive thru menu at your favorite restaurant? Well, I did, and there are at least 70 or more items. That's a lot of choices. As you get to the menu and the voice blares from the little box, "May I take your order?" do you ever feel pressured to make a decision? Can you really decide in just a few short seconds? Maybe you can, but sometimes I like to view the menu for new items and promotions so that I can get the best deal.

If there was ever a great product tester, it would be my mother. My mother is always the first to try new products, especially food items. Are you willing to try new items in the menu of life, or are you stuck in a rut and unable to get out?

There are many options on the menu, but not all are good. Some things in life may be very tasty, but could be unhealthy for you in the long run. You have to be careful as you view the menu of life to make sure the items you choose match your core values and beliefs. Things will come your way that you will never expect, but how you react to them is what counts.

At 22 I was told I had cancer. That was something I did not anticipate on my menu of life. I had to deal with it in a very personal way. I made a decision to look at this pause in my life as a blessing to help me evaluate what I valued most. During those days I took time to write and reflect on what was most important. Since my battle with cancer I look at life differently. I view life as if I received a new lease, but I don't know how long I have. No one does. One reason I am writing this book is because I have no promise of tomorrow; the menu of life could change today.

Action Items

The menu of life can change in a second and everything will be different. So take a moment and review your current menu.

My Current Menu of Life Items

1.)

2.)

Action Items

Are there changes you want to make on your menu board?

If so, write down your new items, and take off a few you want to get rid of.

My New Menu of Life Items

1.)

2.)

"Life is ten percent what happens to you and ninety percent how you respond to it."

Lou Holtz

The Menu 17

Chapter 4

May I Take Your Order?

"*In the long run, we shape our lives, and we shape ourselves. The process never ends until we die. And the choices we make are ultimately our own responsibility.*"

Eleanor Roosevelt

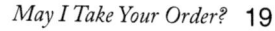

We've jumped into the car, driven to the restaurant, viewed the menu, and now we have to make a choice.

Step one foot into The Varsity, a popular fast foot restaurant in Atlanta, and you will be bombarded by this phrase from all the cashiers: "What'll ya have?" In other words, for all you non-Southerners, they're asking "May I take your order?"

If we order a hamburger, fries, drink, milkshake and a dessert for every meal, that would be a bad choice, right? We need a healthy variety. In life, we make many choices; some great, some good, some bad, and some horrible. But in order to continue moving forward in the drive thru, we must make a choice.

The menu of life is full of choices; we have to make sure we are making the right ones. It is good to mix up your choices so you do not find yourself doing the same thing over and over again. It is important in life to view the menu board and find items that will allow you to better yourself and others. Everyday is full of choices: get up early, workout, sleep in, call a friend, read a book, watch TV, tell a lie, tell the truth, give a gift, take a gift, start a business, close a business, get married, get a divorce… so many choices in life can be overwhelming at times.

Some ingredients that will help you make great choices from life's menu are:

- Pray for wisdom / guidance
- Get counsel from people you respect / Find people who will tell the truth, not give lip service
- Be okay with change / Your decision may require you to do some thing different
- Be Decisive / Not making a choice is making a choice

Once you make a choice, give it everything you have in order to achieve the result you desire.

When I was in college, a very small decision I made had a great impact on my life. At my school, students were required to live on campus unless you were 22 years old or had a doctor's note. Well, my allergies allowed me to get that doctor's note and I lived off campus my senior year. On campus, there were Resident Assistants, or RA's. They lived in the dorms to make sure the students followed all of the rules. One of their responsibilities was to make sure you attended church every Sunday morning (I attended a Christian university). Off campus, there were no RA's, so church became a choice; it wasn't mandatory, and I didn't have anyone making me go. But, I made a choice to go.

That decision had a profound impact on my life. You see, the gentleman that hired me out of college called my landlord. Wow! How he got that number, I'll never know. He asked him some questions, like, "Does he pay his rent on time?" or "What kind of person is he?" But the most important question was this: "Does Robert get up on Sunday mornings and go to church?" He wanted to know if I practiced what I preached, and if I was a man of my word. Because of that he hired me; it started me on a path that allowed me meet important people along the way and eventually start my own company.

Every choice we make in life will have an impact on the timeline of life. One great thing about the drive thru experience is that once you get to the window, you can still change your order. The same applies in life; we can make a choice, but we can also make adjustments to our choice. There is always an opportunity to make a change and to start anew. It is never too late to do that. Life is a timeline, and we need to live as though we are filling the timeline and not just living for another day. All of our choices should be made with the perspective of the past, present, and future, knowing our choices influence others positively and negatively.

Action Items

What choices are you struggling with today?

Write down the advantages and disadvantages to each choice.

This will help you move ahead and make the right choice.

Choice	Advantages	Disadvantages

"It's not hard to make decisions when you know what your values are."

Roy Disney

May I Take Your Order? 23

Chapter 5

Waiting in Line

*A patient man has great understanding,
but a quick-tempered man displays folly.*

Proverbs 14:29

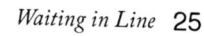

Have you ever been in the drive thru and wondered if the person in front of you was ordering for an entire baseball team because it was taking so long? Or have you ever zipped through the drive thru only to get to the window and have the customer service person tell you to pull ahead because your order isn't ready yet? Well, I hope *all* of those scenarios have happened to you, because I would feel bad if I was the only one with those experiences. I'm joking of course, but doesn't it seem like the smallest and most trivial things get under our skin, especially when we're in a hurry?

That's why I wanted to talk about patience. It's a true sign of success. Why? Well, patience teaches us a lot of things. Think about some products you enjoy. Take a moment and research how long it took them to start making money after the idea was conceived. Many small companies take three to five years to make a profit. ESPN, a giant in cable television, did not turn a profit until six years after going on the air. Just look at them now! As of the third fiscal quarter of 2009 for The Walt Disney Company (which owns ESPN), the media networks division reports a 1.3 billion profit (Figure includes ABC and Disney Networks). Good things can come to those who wait!

Patience can also be very frustrating if you are waiting for a business deal, or awaiting team cuts, layoffs, or waiting for your child to be born because you are so excited and just can't wait. I have written many proposals and given many presentations only to be told "no" or "wait." However, I have found that you learn more through failure, defeat, disappointment, trials, and/or experiences than you do through instant success. Besides, does it really pay to be impatient? Think about some of the results of impatience: restlessness, irritability, anger, being difficult to get along with, etc... which are all for nothing, because you will still have to wait either way. Therefore, the wait can be long or short, but it requires patience.

As an NFL agent, you recruit players and start introducing yourself about 10 months before they can sign with you. I spend time getting to know them, showing them they are important to me and my firm. I also spend countless hours helping them see the value my company offers over other firms. After a player's last game, I am allowed to ask if they will be signing with our firm, US Sports. After all of that time, energy and relationship building, they still may choose another firm. It requires an unbelievable amount of patience.

So the next time the person at the drive thru window says, "Pull up, your order is not ready," remember that the wait is only about three to five minutes, not 10 months. So be patient, because your food will be good and hot.

Action Items

Think of three different situations where you can improve your patience.

1.)

2.)

3.)

Now write down how you will improve each item above.

1.)

2.)

3.)

"Patience is the companion of wisdom."

Saint Augustine

Chapter 6

The Window

"Do to others as you would have them do to you."

Jesus (Luke 6:31)

Is this the longest drive thru you have ever been to? Well, we are finally here at the window. Now we can see the busyness as they prepare the food. That is a beautiful thing; so many people working together as a team to produce great products in such a short period of time. The person at the window is critical. They are the face of your franchise. They are the last thing people remember about your place of business.

Have you ever thought about who is the face of your business, occupation, family or your very own brand? You are! The window represents help, as someone reaches out to give me food my body wants and needs. They take my money, give me change, pass the food to me and make sure I received my order.

We all need to find ways to help people along life's path. If you are totally consumed with self, you will find no one reaching out for you when you need assistance. Find ways to help someone everyday of your life. It can be as simple as holding a door open, carrying a package, or visiting with an elderly widow. Take a moment to spot someone who needs a hand. Let them know that you are willing and would love to help them with their needs. You could even surprise them one day by showing up on their doorstep, ready to offer a helping hand.

In 1988, I took time to help former NBA Champion and All-Star

Bobby Jones. We were working together when I was an athletic director. He came into my office one day and said, "I'm getting a lot of requests for speaking, appearances, and endorsements. Could you help me with this? I need someone to call these people and work on an agreement." I had never represented a celebrity or tried to negotiate a contract for their services, but I agreed to help him and it worked out well for both of us. He received a great contract and I received the blessing of helping and learning something new. Little did I know that this was the beginning of a new journey for me. I began representing him and he quickly introduced me to other athletes, including Basketball Hall of Famer David Thompson, who we also represent. That was the start of US Sports, which has been in business for more than two decades.

Another quality the person at the window should represent is kindness. When I think of kindness, I'm reminded of something you were likely taught at an early age – the golden rule, which says "Do to others as you would have them do unto you." Webster's Dictionary defines the word "kind" as: "sympathetic, friendly, gentle, tenderhearted, and generous." Being kind to someone is so simple, but we often don't take the opportunity to do it. I believe we should all find ways to spread a little kindness. It doesn't cost anything. All we have to do is smile or say, "How are you today?" then actually wait to hear their response.

I'm sure you can remember a time when you were a bit down and someone showed you kindness. How did that make you feel? It probably encouraged you to know that someone cared. It's always good to treat others as you would like to be treated. A little kindness can go a long way.

In my line of work, traveling is often necessary. During one trip, I needed to stop somewhere. It was 2:30 a.m. I had been driving from a recruiting visit, and I was exhausted. I checked into a hotel, went to my room and fell asleep. The next morning, I went downstairs for breakfast. The lady helping with the breakfast seemed so pleasant and kind. We chatted and I told her I enjoyed her music (she was listening to some contemporary Christian music). She began to tell me the story of the night before. A gentleman checked in, just like me, wearing a suit and tie. It was 2:30a.m., he had been driving for hours, and the hotel desk clerk said the man looked distraught and unhappy. He went upstairs to his room, sat down on the floor and shot himself in the head. The lady working the hotel breakfast said, "I wish I could have just shared a kind word. It may have made a difference in his life."

We never know how much our words can affect people in a positive way. It takes work to be aware of the needs around us, but it can make all the difference in the world.

Action Items

Think of two people you can reach out to. There's no agenda or monetary reward for you, just a helping hand.

1.)

2.)

Now as you reach out, what kind of service or assistance can you provide?

1.)

2.)

Action Items

Now think about people you come in contact with each day. Consider ways you can show them kindness. Also, think of ways that you can show kindness to people you come in contact with and *don't* know.

List four ways you can show kindness to people.

1.)

2.)

3.)

4.)

"Kind words can be short and easy to speak, but their echoes are truly endless."

Mother Teresa

Chapter 7

Here's Your Order

"Few things help an individual more than to place responsibility upon him, and to let him know that you trust him."

Booker T. Washington

We are now at the window and they hand us our food. This is a great feeling. Finally, I have received what I got in line for – my food. Oh, but wait a minute, how do I know I have my order? How do I know if I received the right amount of straws, napkins, drinks, food and other items? Sometimes there is so much pressure to move ahead that you don't even look to check your order. I call it "Drive Thru Trust."

I have often marveled at how the workers consistently do such a great job getting the orders right and keeping the lines moving. I believe if there was a high percentage of lost or bad orders received by customers, the line would really slow down as people checked and double-checked their orders. I think you would have drive thru rage by everyone waiting on each other to check their bags. Trust, though, is why the line moves ahead quickly. We trust our order is correct and move on down the road.

In our quest to find true success, we must trust so many people. Have you ever stopped to think of all the people you trust on a daily basis? I did. Look at this list:

- My son's and daughter's coaches
- The driver on the other side of me
- The driver who is coming at me or on the other side of the road

- My son's and daughter's teachers
- The school administrator and employees
- My co-workers
- My athletes
- My athletes' coaches

- My friends
- My banker
- My neighbor
- My wife and kids
- My accountant

I will stop there. That is simply people you trust daily, not counting all the people you need to trust weekly, monthly, quarterly and yearly. So I think we can all agree, trust is a critical element to success. If we spent all our time worrying about things, we would never be successful. Trust takes an investment of time and energy. You must invest into the relationship to gain the trust of someone.

I saw something about a topic that is sweeping the country called "Stop the Snitching." Basically, if you see something wrong, no matter what it is, stealing or even murder – whatever you do, do not tell who did it; don't snitch. So basically there is no rule of law, no trust between family, friends and neighbors. Without trust in life and business, there will be no peace.

Being the publisher of Sports Spectrum magazine, an NFL agent, and overseeing our sports management company, I have to trust so many people. I have accountants, attorneys, controllers, editors, graphic designers, printers, writers, players... if someone decided to steal or not perform, I am in trouble. But I learned that trust is key. Hire good people, recruit great players with values, get out of the way and let them do their job.

While making a choice to trust a person, it is a good idea to check their background and do your due diligence. Investors trusted Bernard Madoff to invest their money in his investment company. Instead of investing the money, Madoff deposited it into his bank account while making up fraudulent trading statements to cover his tracks. He stole a reported 65 billion dollars. Many individuals and companies lost huge amounts of money. So while we can trust the person at the window with our food, we should be careful with whom we trust in life.

Action Items

Who do you trust and why?

Name / Why?

1.)

2.)

3.)

Who can you build a better trusting relationship with and how? What are the benefits of that trust?

Name

How?

Benefits

"Trust, but verify."

Ronald Reagan

Chapter 8

When eating bamboo sprouts, remember the man who planted them.

Chinese Proverb

We are now at a critical moment. Do we say, "Thank you and have a nice day," or do we just snatch our food and drive away? Maybe you've had a frustrating drive thru experience, but should that bad experience equal a bad attitude? The person handing you the food probably played little, if any, part in your bad experience.

Have you ever noticed how a 2, 3, 4 or 5-year-old child does such a great job of saying "thank you" when you give them something? But then, as they get older, it seems to fade away. I believe the reason is because of our daily example in front of children. If we want children to grow up with a thankful heart, we need to set a great example.

Think of times that you have been ungrateful to people. Did you think only of your needs and wants, or did you consider theirs? Life is full of opportunity. The question is, what will you do with it? I have chosen to say "thank you" during the weekend of the NFL draft; I call each of my current NFL clients and say "thank you" for allowing me to work on their behalf. It is a yearly reminder that lets them know I appreciate the trust they have in me. Whatever your occupation, the phrase "thank you" costs you nothing, but it does have a great return on the investment.

As you build relationships with others, remember that people will always try to help you if they see that you appreciate their work and efforts. A good example of that is John Wooden, the Hall of Fame basketball coach, who won 10 National Championships at UCLA.

If you ever watch video or read about his players, you will see they loved their coach and appreciated his efforts to make them better at life and basketball, and he appreciated their efforts as well. Bill Walton, who played at UCLA for Wooden, said this about his coach: "Coach Wooden is a humble, private man who has selflessly given up his life to make other's lives better… It is never about him…"

I believe the love of a coach, CEO, parent, etc. is the best motivator for people to give their very best day in and day out. If you never let people know you are grateful and thankful for their work and effort, count on low performance. If you want high performance, praise your team, employees, or family members and let them know you are thankful for their dedication to the task, whatever that may be.

Action Items

List three ways you can show or tell people you are thankful.

1.)

2.)

3.)

List at least three people you need to touch with thankfulness.

1.)

2.)

3.)

Think of someone who impacted your life greatly. Send them a personal, hand-written note and say thank you.

"As we express our gratitude, we must never forget that the highest appreciation is not to utter words, but to live by them."

John F. Kennedy

Thank You!

Chapter 9

Oops! Too Much Change

"Character is like a tree and reputation like its shadow. The shadow is what we think of it; the tree is the real thing."

Abraham Lincoln

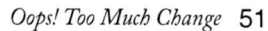

Have you ever been through the drive thru and received extra fries, an extra sandwich, or extra change or cash? What did you do? Did you take it back or just keep going and say, "Wow! That was really great! I got an extra sandwich."

The depth of person shows up when we are alone. When no one is looking we have to make the right choice. You know the right choice; the question is whether you will make the right choice.

One day, after visiting my son at school for lunch, I asked his teacher if there was anything his class needed. She told me they could use new balls for the playground. So I made a trip to the store and purchased balls, a pump, needles and a crate to hold the balls. As I put everything in the car, I noticed that the needles were lying underneath the balls at the bottom of the crate. It crossed my mind that I had not been charged for the needles. So I checked the receipt, and sure enough I had not been charged. I was in a big hurry and had to get back to work. It was just a .79 cent package of needles, right? It would have been the convenient choice to just drive away, but I knew what the right choice was; march back into the store and pay for the needles. So I did.

In life, we will continually be challenged with issues regarding character and integrity. When the challenge comes, make the right choice, no matter the consequence. So it starts at the drive thru. If we cannot do the right thing there, we will stumble in our quest to show people our life and business have character and integrity. There is a simple saying, "If you cannot be honest with the little things, do not expect to oversee bigger things in your life."

In our firm, US Sports, we have what we call "Tru Rewards". Part of this program is about an open book policy; which means that at any time my client can come into my office and ask to look at their individual files and financial numbers related to agreements and compensation. At the time of publishing, I believe we are the only firm to offer this service to our clients. What can happen in the sports management and marketing business is that firms will charge a high price for the athlete's service, but pay the athlete a much lower amount. For example, a firm will charge $10,000 for an athlete appearance. The firm knows the athlete will take $5,000, so the athlete does not get the total gross fee. Instead the firm pockets $5,000. If the firm managed their business according to character and integrity, the firm would offer $10,000 to the athlete with the athlete then paying the firm 10-20 percent of the total gross fee as a service back to the firm. I am very thankful to say our firm has great people that help maintain our brand at US Sports and always make the right choice even if it may cost us money and time.

Character and integrity will carry you a long way in life. Remember when we talked about the timeline of life? Well, live for that timeline and do not become the person who just lives for the moment with no end in sight.

Action Items

Can someone question your business or personal life in regards to character and integrity? List 5 qualities of what good character and integrity mean to you?

1.)

2.)

3.)

4.)

5.)

Which of the above qualities can be seen in your life daily?

Which qualities can you improve on? How?

"Be more concerned with your character than your reputation, because your character is what you really are, while your reputation is merely what others think you are."

John Wooden

Chapter 10

Drive Away

"Die when I may, I want it said of me by those who knew me best, that I always plucked a thistle and planted a flower where I thought a flower would grow."

Abraham Lincoln

Now that you are exiting the drive thru with happiness and joy because you have what you came for (the food), how will you be remembered?

In life, we should live everyday with an attitude that I may drive away today and never be seen again. It could be your last day here on Earth. Are you ready? How and what will people remember you by? Will it be your good character traits that grant you *Drive Thru Success*, or will it be for something else? And if so, what might that be?

Have you ever wished you could be around to hear what everybody would say about you at your funeral? Well, we all know that can't happen. What if there was an open microphone at your funeral for people to say anything they wanted? What would your family hear?

I want to challenge you to live out the *Drive Thru Success* model everyday in your life. When it is time to drive away, people will say you were a person with *Drive Thru Success* qualities, that you made a difference in life by living out these simple principles on a daily basis.

From the moment you jump into the car until the moment that you exit the drive thru, the choices belong to you. There are other players whom you will interact with, but they cannot make your decisions. In fact, it is your choice whether the actions of others will influence your reactions.

If you wait until the moment hits to make your decisions, success will be hard to reach. Poor choices are easier to make when there is no plan in place. A stiff wind will blow you around when you are not prepared for the conditions. The principles in this brief book are meant to help you prepare for the journey ahead – ready to face the challenges that lie to come with a firm grasp of how to get there.

So that brings us to the conclusion of this book and the starting line of your journey. By reading this far, you have participated in a process, learning what it will take to be successful. Go out there and do it. If you hit a bump in the road, stop back in for a quick refresher and then get back out there. The reward at the end is worth the work.

Action Items

When I drive away, what do I want people to say about me?

Is that what people would say today? If not, what can you do to change that?

"I hope I shall possess firmness and virtue enough to maintain what I consider the most enviable of all titles, the character of an honest man."

George Washington

DRIVE THRU
STEPS TO SUCCESS

Exit Here

"Success is peace of mind which is a direct result of self-satisfaction in knowing you did your best to become the best you are capable of becoming."

John Wooden

YOUR ORDER IS NOW READY

10 ITEMS FOR SUCCESS

1 – Jump In – **Do not be afraid!**

2 – The Ride – **Free Repairs Open 24/7 No Appointment Necessary: God's Repair Shop**

3 – The Menu – **Be willing to take time to view all the options in life.**

4 – May I Take Your Order? – **Be strong enough to accept a bad choice, change and move on.**

5 – Waiting in Line – **Remember patience is a breeding ground for success.**

6 – The Window – **Be kind, and always be willing to offer a helping hand.**

7 – Here's Your Order – **Build relationships on trust and honor. Do not be afraid to review that trust from time to time.**

8 – Thank You! – How many ways can you say thank you?

9 – Oops! Too Much Change – Character and Integrity are the foundation of who you are everyday.

10- Drive Away – What kind of impression will you leave behind? What will people remember you by?

DRIVE THRU SUCCESS EXTRA

Renewing the Mind

We have all been programmed by the way we were raised, and we have been influenced in subtle ways by our co-workers, neighbors, friends and family. However, we can change the way we think by renewing our mind.

It's a simple concept that allows us to put more good into our mind than bad. We have many negative influences and influencers in our life. People saying, you can't do this, or you can't do that, or that you'll never make it, etc. But if you review the 10 items for success and memorize one quote per week, you will find that your mind has been renewed, and you will believe and achieve what God has created you to do. So to continue your journey with *Drive Thru Success,* read and memorize one quote per week for 52 weeks (one year). Send me an e-mail, Tweet at drivethrusucces (only one 's' at the end, Twitter has a character limit), or visit the website at **www.drivethrusuccess.com** to let me know what *Drive Thru Success* has meant to you and your family's life.

Thank you for reading *Drive Thru Success*. It means more to me to give you this experience than you will ever know. I pray that your success will be great and that the change in your life will be transparent so that others will see you have *Drive Thru Success*.

Week 1

"Nothing can stop the man with the right mental attitude from achieving his goal; nothing on earth can help the man with the wrong mental attitude."

Thomas Jefferson

☐ *Quote Completed*   *Date Completed*

Week 2

"Don't give up. Don't ever give up."

Jim Valvano

☐ *Quote Completed*   *Date Completed*

Week 3

"We keep moving forward, opening new doors, and doing new things, because we're curious and curiosity keeps leading us down new paths."

Walt Disney

☐ *Quote Completed*   *Date Completed*

Week 4

"When one bases his life on principle, 99 percent of his decisions are already made."
Author Unknown

☐ *Quote Completed* ∽ *Date Completed* [   ]

Week 5

"He that can have patience can have what he will"
Benjamin Franklin

☐ *Quote Completed* ∽ *Date Completed* [   ]

Week 6

"Kindness is the language which the deaf can hear and the blind can see."
Mark Twain

☐ *Quote Completed* ∽ *Date Completed* [   ]

Week 7

"Trust men and they will be true to you; treat them greatly and they will show themselves great."

Ralph Waldo Emerson

☐ *Quote Completed*   ∽   *Date Completed*

Week 8

"There is always, always, always something to be thankful for."

Author Unknown

☐ *Quote Completed*   ∽   *Date Completed*

Week 9

Finally, brothers, whatever is true, whatever is noble, whatever is right, whatever is pure, whatever is lovely, whatever is admirable—if anything is excellent or praiseworthy—think about such things.

Philippians 4:8

☐ *Quote Completed*   ∽   *Date Completed*

Week 10

"My hope still is to leave the world a bit better than when I got here."
Jim Henson

☐ *Quote Completed*   *Date Completed*

Week 11

Lazy hands make a man poor, but diligent hands bring wealth.
Proverbs 10:4

☐ *Quote Completed*   *Date Completed*

Week 12

"All mankind is divided into three classes: those that are immovable, those that are movable, and those that move."
Benjamin Franklin

☐ *Quote Completed*   *Date Completed*

Week 13

"Never give in, never give in, never; never; never; never - in nothing, great or small, large or petty - never give in except to convictions of honor and good sense"
Winston Churchill

☐ *Quote Completed*   *Date Completed*

Week 14

"Show me someone who has done something worthwhile, and I'll show you someone who has overcome adversity."
Lou Holtz

☐ *Quote Completed*   *Date Completed*

Week 15

"It's not hard to make decisions when you know what your values are."
Roy Disney

☐ *Quote Completed*   *Date Completed*

Week 16

"Patience is the companion of wisdom."
Saint Augustine

☐ *Date Completed* ≈ *Verse Completed*

Week 17

*9 Two are better than one,
because they have a good return for their work:
10 If one falls down,
his friend can help him up.
But pity the man who falls
and has no one to help him up!*
Ecclesiastes 4:9-10

☐ *Date Completed* ≈ *Verse Completed*

Week 18

"Trust, but verify."
Ronald Reagan

☐ *Date Completed* ≈ *Verse Completed*

Week 19

"The Pilgrims made seven times more graves than huts. No Americans have been more impoverished than these who, nevertheless, set aside a day of thanksgiving."

H.U. Westermayer

☐ *Date Completed* ∽ *Verse Completed*

Week 20

"Be more concerned with your character than your reputation, because your character is what you really are, while your reputation is merely what others think you are."

John Wooden

☐ *Date Completed* ∽ *Verse Completed*

Week 21

"Die when I may, I want it said of me by those who knew me best, that I always plucked a thistle and planted a flower where I thought a flower would grow."

Abraham Lincoln

☐ *Date Completed* ∽ *Verse Completed*

Extra: Renewing The Mind

Week 22

"Build up your weaknesses until they become your strong points."
Knute Rockne

☐ *Quote Completed*   ∽   *DateCompleted*

Week 23

"It is hard to fail, but it is worse never to have tried to succeed."
Theodore Roosevelt

☐ *Quote Completed*   ∽   *Date Completed*

Week 24

"The greater danger for most of us lies not in setting our aim too high and falling short; but in setting our aim too low, and achieving our mark."
Michelangelo

☐ *Quote Completed*   ∽   *Date Completed*

Week 25

"Don't fear failure so much that you refuse to try new things. The saddest summary of a life contains three descriptions: could have, might have, and should have."

Louis E. Boone

☐ *Quote Completed*   *Date Completed* [　　　　　]

Week 26

"Treasure your relationships, not your possessions."

Anthony J. D'Angelo

☐ *Quote Completed*   *Date Completed* [　　　　　]

Week 27

"In the long run, we shape our lives, and we shape ourselves. The process never ends until we die. And the choices we make are ultimately our own responsibility."

Eleanor Roosevelt

☐ *Quote Completed*   *Date Completed* [　　　　　]

Week 28

A patient man has great understanding, but a quick-tempered man displays folly.
Proverbs 14:29

☐ *Quote Completed*   ⇜   *Date Completed* []

Week 29

"Kind words can be short and easy to speak, but their echoes are truly endless."
Mother Teresa

☐ *Quote Completed*   ⇜   *Date Completed* []

Week 30

"Few things help an individual more than to place responsibility upon him, and to let him know that you trust him."
Booker T. Washington

☐ *Quote Completed*   ⇜   *Date Completed* []

Week 31

When eating bamboo sprouts, remember the man who planted them.
Chinese Proverb

☐ *Quote Completed*   *Date Completed*

Week 32

"Character is like a tree and reputation like its shadow. The shadow is what we think of it; the tree is the real thing."
Abraham Lincoln

☐ *Quote Completed*   *Date Completed*

Week 33

"I hope I shall possess firmness and virtue enough to maintain what I consider the most enviable of all titles, the character of an honest man."
George Washington

☐ *Quote Completed*   *Date Completed*

Week 34

"Don't go around saying the world owes you a living. The world owes you nothing. It was here first."
Mark Twain

☐ *Quote Completed*   ≈   *Date Completed* ⬚

Week 35

"You may be disappointed if you fail, but you are doomed if you don't try."
Beverly Sills

☐ *Quote Completed*   ≈   *Date Completed* ⬚

Week 36

"Success isn't permanent and failure isn't fatal."
Mike Ditka

☐ *Quote Completed*   ≈   *Date Completed* ⬚

Week 37

"How do you go from where you are to where you wanna be? And I think you have to have an enthusiasm for life. You have to have a dream, a goal. And you have to be willing to work for it."

Jim Valvano

☐ *Quote Completed*   *Date Completed*

Week 38

"Trials are medicines which our gracious and wise physician subscribes, because we need them; and he proportions the frequency and weight of them to what the case requires. Let us trust his skill and thank him for his prescription."

Isaac Newton

☐ *Quote Completed*   *Date Completed*

Week 39

"Life is ten percent what happens to you and ninety percent how you respond to it."

Lou Holtz

☐ *Quote Completed*   *Date Completed*

Week 40

"A life spent making mistakes is not only more honorable, but more useful than a life spent doing nothing."
George Bernard Shaw

☐ *Quote Completed*   ～   *Date Completed*

Week 41

"Consult not your fears but your hopes and your dreams. Think not about your frustrations, but about your unfulfilled potential. Concern yourself not with what you tried and failed in, but with what it is still possible for you to do."
Pope John XXIII

☐ *Quote Completed*   ～   *Date Completed*

Week 42

"Wherever there is a human being there is an opportunity for a kindness."
Lucius Annaeus Seneca

☐ *Quote Completed*   ～   *Date Completed*

Week 43

"There are no secrets to success. It is the result of preparation, hard work, and learning from failure."

Colin Powell

☐ *Quote Completed* ~ *Date Completed* [＿＿＿＿＿]

Week 44

"As we express our gratitude, we must never forget that the highest appreciation is not to utter words, but to live by them."

John F. Kennedy

☐ *Quote Completed* ~ *Date Completed* [＿＿＿＿＿]

Week 45

"A man should never neglect his family for business."

Walt Disney

☐ *Quote Completed* ~ *Date Completed* [＿＿＿＿＿]

Extra: Renewing The Mind

Week 46

"Never leave that till tomorrow which you can do today."

Benjamin Franklin

☐ *Quote Completed*   ✎   *Date Completed* [   ]

Week 47

"Love all, trust a few, do wrong to none."

William Shakespeare

☐ *Quote Completed*   ✎   *Date Completed* [   ]

Week 48

"Some people dream of success... while others wake up and work hard at it."

Author Unknown

☐ *Quote Completed*   ✎   *Date Completed* [   ]

Week 49

"Do to others as you would have them do to you."

Jesus (Luke 6:31)

☐ *Quote Completed*   ✎   *Date Completed* [   ]

Week 50

"Success consists of going from failure to failure without loss of enthusiasm."
Winston Churchill

☐ *Quote Completed* ～ *Date Completed*

Week 51

"Success is peace of mind which is a direct result of self-satisfaction in knowing you did your best to become the best you are capable of becoming."
John Wooden

☐ *Quote Completed* ～ *Date Completed*

Week 52

"I firmly believe that any man's finest hour, the greatest fulfillment of all that he holds dear, is the moment when he has worked his heart out in a good cause and lies exhausted on the field of battle – victorious"
Vince Lombardi

☐ *Quote Completed* ～ *Date Completed*

ABOUT THE AUTHOR

Robert Walker (B.S. Physical Education, Masters Sports Management) is the President and CEO of Unlimited Success Sports Management Inc. (www.ussportsmanagement.com), a full-service sports management firm representing current NFL players as their agent, as well as full-service marketing and branding for athletes and companies and the publisher of *Sports Spectrum* magazine (www.sportsspectrum.com), which has been celebrating "the good in sports" for more than 25 years. Robert received a B.S. in Physical Education from Liberty University and then went on to the United States Sports Academy, earning his Masters in Sports Management.

A love of sports and athletes has been the groundwork for Robert's professional career. He served on the boards for both Fellowship of Christian Athletes (FCA Charlotte) and Sports Outreach America (SOA). He spent many years developing athletes and shaping lives as a coach. Products of his coaching efforts include many NCAA Division I basketball players, one NBA player, and two State Championship teams. During these coaching years, he was also the Athletic Director for two schools.

Robert left his role as Athletic Director in 1994 to expand into a fulltime enterprise in sports management.

He has spoken to numerous groups and made appearances on television and radio. He is also the author of *ADvantage*, a 300 plus page manual to help train and develop Athletic Directors. Robert's new book, *Living the Thankful Life*, will be coming to stores soon.

On a more personal note, Robert resides in North Carolina with his wife and their two children, and is an active member at his local church. Robert is also passionate about bringing change to Sudan, through the humanitarian efforts of *With Open Eyes*. To learn more go to www.withopeneyes.net

READER'S QUOTES

"What a great way to relate the basic principles of success! Robert lays out simple and easy to understand principles that so many of us are quick to relate to. The Drive Away chapter was particularly interesting to me. How important is it to think about the impression we leave on those we may never see again!"

Dr. Steven A. Jirgal
Pastor

"Achieving success is a high priority for a lot of people. In just 30 minutes you can learn 10 principles that can be applied to every aspect of your life. Read them, use them, live by them."

Crystal Rhodes
Charleston Southern University Hall of Fame

"Robert gives us profound yet practical ways to address issues and lay a solid foundation for a brighter tomorrow. Though I value the entire book, I have found the chapters on patience and decision-making to be of immense value and wisdom. Challenging, yet inspirational, *Drive Thru Success* gives us a modern outline to becoming all that God created us to be."

Mike Metcalf Jr.
2008 Pit Crew Champion

"I have known Robert Walker for over 20 years and have always appreciated his creativity, optimism, and desire to serve our Lord. This book is a true reflection of his outlook on life and his desire to make the most of every situation he encounters. The simplicity of the book and the perspective from which it is written, provide a breath of fresh air for the reader."

Dr. Alan Geist
Athletic Director

"Very creative. Simple but thought provoking. An enjoyable read. One thing that stood out to me was the Thank You chapter, because it reminded me of something I need to do more often."

Jennifer Zurawick, M.D.
Pediatrician

"Great book! The Action Items at the end of each chapter really help with life application. This would be a great gift for students who are in the process of goal setting."

Amber Smith
Education Coordinator

"Drive Thru Success is a highly interactive book that relates to my everyday life. It not only tells you the steps involved, but helps you assess where you are now, and how to successfully 'drive thru' and achieve your goals while helping others along the way."

Nicole Payne
Financial Controller

"I want to buy copies for my race crew! It gives a great map for this 'sound bite,' 'headline' generation. Thanks for writing this book!"

Cal Huge
Retiree